ENLIGHTENMENT

心道法師系列 04

心靈舞蹈 Mind Ballet

發行人◎徐玉珠
作者◎心道法師
繪圖◎尤傳賢
英譯◎許國華
責任編輯◎初沾衣·周掌宇
版面構成◎兩隻老虎廣告設計有限公司

出版者◎財團法人靈鷲山般若文教基金會附設出版社
地址◎台北市南京東路五段 92 號 9 樓
讀者服務專線◎ 2760-3881 轉 627
郵撥帳號◎ 18887793
戶名◎財團法人靈鷲山般若文教基金會附設出版社
統一編號◎ 78359502
編輯部◎台北市南京東路五段 92 號 5 樓
電話◎（02）2760-3881
傳真◎（02）2768-4550

印刷者◎英勇股份有限公司
電話◎（02）3234-1961
發行日期◎ 2001 年 11 月
印刷版次◎初版一刷
定價◎ 200 元

心靈
Mind Ballet
舞蹈

作者◎心道法師 Master Hsin Tao

繪圖◎尤傳賢 YUSHA

英譯◎許國華 Hsu Kuo-Hua

心，在那裡？

　　每個人都有一顆可以自由舞蹈的心，但是有的人的心被關住了，有的人的心睡著了，有的人的心不見了，最有趣的是大部份的時候我們還不知道自己有「心」。

　　你一定不同意，一個人怎麼可能不知道自己有「心」呢？

　　這真是個好反問，不過，我可回答不了這個問題，因為我也覺得我有一顆心，它會哭會笑，有喜怒哀樂，它明明存在怎說我不知道它的存在？

　　我這樣子活了很久，覺得自己過得很清楚很明白。直到有一天，我看見一個人(是活人，不是書上的人)，他的氣度風采讓我困惑！在他身上有股神秘的靜定力量，不論外在環境像雲霄飛車一樣的驟起驟落，他總是笑瞇瞇地，沒事兒人般地處理著，行所當行，言所當言。對於發生在自己身上的橫逆，不但不怨，反而還有餘裕再給別人些什麼！於是我發揮好奇的天性，研究這個人為何有此力量？結果發現，他的秘密武器居然是因為他知道他有「心」！但是，他也沒辦法把這個「心」拿給我看看，我只能在自己身上找，………多令人失望的答案！不過，起碼我知道有這麼顆我不認識的「心」值得去找找。

　　如果，你也像我一樣的好奇，想了解這「心」的力量，翻翻心道法師的這本《心靈舞蹈》吧！這是一個過來人告訴你他自己的經驗。可別急嘛！你越積極去找就越找不到，因為聽說這顆心要用「無心」去找，不過，不積極也不行，……我說的話你是不是愈聽愈糊塗了？沒關係，疑問愈多愈好，有疑問就表示你上路了，遲早會找到你的那顆常在身邊，卻不曾照過面的「心」！

城邦橡樹林出版社總編輯

禪機要怎麼去懂？

　　我對寫字雖然有幾分天資，平常卻很少練字，通常是有人跟我求字時才寫。也可以說是跟我求字的人在幫我練字了，所以是該他謝我還是我謝他呢？可見事情確實很難只從片面去看。

　　別人請我寫字時，我最愛寫即興的話。所以寫得好不好（包括寫的字和寫的話）就要看當時的心境靈感而定。如果氣機流動，就話好字也好；如果生命凝滯，字也會木然，話就更像教條了。

　　寫字的我尤其喜歡請求字者提一個字或兩個字，如「靜」、「樂」、「誠實」、「喜歡」等等，我就即席感應，隨手寫些小字，布置在那一、兩個大字下面，以為詮釋。就像鄭板橋在「難得糊塗」下面，寫了「聰明難，糊塗難，由聰明轉入糊塗更難……」一段話以為引申一樣。往往也真的福至心靈，直說到求字者的心坎裡，那就算是件成功的作品了。所謂成功，不止是指那一幅字，更是指人我間一點生命氣機的交流哩！

　　曾有一次，有人請我寫一個「禪」字。在這一個大大的禪字之下，我信手寫下如此這般一句話：「禪就是什麼都不是，連禪都不是。」

　　這算不算是我心偶然觸機的悟道之言呢？也許是，如果我當時果真心誠且明。也許不是，如果我只是掉弄機鋒。也許曾經是轉眼又不是，如果我悟後便為此沾沾自喜……而如今看來，恐怕老早已不是了，因為我竟然至今還記得這句話沒有適時忘掉。

　　禪真是不好懂，因為太滑了。以致我雖然可能曾懂過，也不知所懂的是真是假。所以又怎麼敢為心道法師這本禪書作序呢？都因編者力催，才不得已胡謅應命，算不算序也不知道，讀者看了可能一頭霧水。但也許不必這麼當真，放鬆心懷，也未嘗不可一笑置之，相悅以解。很可能心道法師這本書就該這樣去看的。心道師父：這樣說可以嗎？

　　　　　　　　　　　　　　　　　　　龔鵬程　淡江大學中文系教授

CONTENTS

心靈舞蹈 *Mind Ballet*

Mind

Ballet

一 ◆ 習性 Habitual Tendencies

生活中經常檢視自己的習慣、妄想，
瞭解真實的你，才能夠慢慢離開假相，
少欲無為，身心自在。

In order to discover your true self, you have to examine
your bad habits and illusory thoughts in the daily life all
the time. That's also the way to wipe out illusory
phenomena, and to lead a blissful and easeful life.

洗鍋子 Washing a Pot

習氣像鍋垢，天天洗，天天乾淨；
天天不洗，想洗就難。

Habitual tendencies are just like a pot that is caked with dried filth. If you wash the pot everyday, you can keep it spotlessly clean. If you don't wash it everyday, it'll be hard to wash the filth off later.

不好的個性放任久了，
就會慢慢養成很大的習氣。

If you give free reign your bad behavior,
it'll gradually become habit-forming.

每個人都有習氣，習氣就像炒菜鍋的油垢一樣，
一天不洗、兩天不洗、三天不洗、一個禮拜不洗，
還能炒菜嗎？

Everybody has habitual tendencies.
Habitual tendencies are just like oil stains on the
frying pan. The sooner you wash the stains off the
better. If you don't clean the frying pan for one day,
two days, three days, one week, or more, the frying
pan will become useless.

鍋子用過後要清洗，洗過就會很乾淨，
如果能夠把油垢的習氣除掉，就不會沾染，
如果沒有常常清洗，就會累積過多習氣，
到最後就成了業氣，
這是一定要輪迴的啊！

You have to wash the pot clean after using it.
If you wash away the 'oil stains' of habitual tendencies, you'll be free of defilements.
If you don't wash the 'stains' frequently, you'll get more and more habitual tendencies. These habitual tendencies will form your karma, which causes reincarnation!

雲與霧 Cloud and Mist

抓住人生目標，認清妄念只是不實際的影像。

Grasp the meaning of life, and realize that illusory thoughts are unfounded.

妄想就像雲與霧一般，一會兒飄到這裡，一會兒飄到那裡，
下一場雨，就無影無蹤，不復存在了。

Illusory thoughts are like cloud and mist, drifting here to there.
However, they both vanish after a heavy rain.

所以對治妄想的辦法，也是這樣：
不去理它就好了。
或是多念佛、打坐，
藉著觀照而透視一切的虛妄，
認清妄想只是一個不真實的影像，
它來了又消失，
重要的是，掌握自己人生的目標：
走向正覺之路。

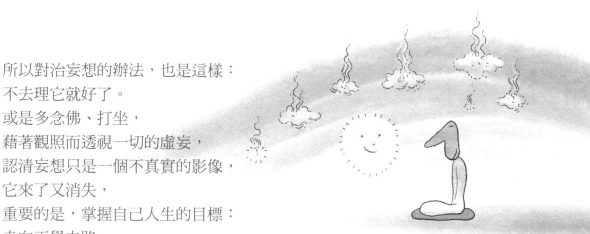

So, what should we do when illusory thoughts arise?
Just pay them no heed!
Maybe you can keep reciting the Buddha's name, or practicing meditation.
With prajna wisdom, you see that all phenomena are unreal, and also realize that all illusory thoughts are dreamlike matter that comes and goes. The most important thing is to grasp the meaning of life, and to walk toward the path of right enlightenment.

挖礦 Mining

除去妄想，才能修鍊成金。

Get rid of illusory thoughts and you can smelt gold successfully.

修行就像挖礦，
除妄想如同銷去雜質，
成金後就不復為礦了。
修行是為了消除習氣，
如果完全除掉了，
就是心空的世界，
自在逍遙。

Spiritual practice is just like mining.
Getting rid of illusory thoughts is very much like removing impurities.
After gold is refined, there is no longer any ore.
In order to do away with habitual tendencies, you need to practice spiritual cultivation.
If you stamp out your habitual tendencies completely, you'll gain the world of emptiness, and will lead a blissful and easeful life.

變身 Metamorphosis

處處是真，處處是假，
所以處處不能貪住才是真的。

Nothing is real. The truth is not clinging.

到底什麼是真正的你呢？

這一世也許是人，但下一世就不知道了；

我們處在這生死輪迴中，就這樣循環不已的變！變！變！

但是，你到底是什麼呢？

Who is the real you?

In this life you are human. However, you don't know what you're going to be in the next life.

Nobody can escape reincarnation of birth and death. Endlessly revolving birth and death, birth and death, and again birth and death!

Nevertheless, what are you really?

事實上，並沒有一個定相是「你」，
也許今天是人，明天是馬，到了後天卻成了一隻飛鼠！
那我到底是馬還是人呢？是飛鼠還是蝴蝶呢？

Actually, 'you' has no solid reality.
You're human right now. But, tomorrow you might be a
horse or the day after tomorrow you might turn into a
flying squirrel.
So, am I a horse or a human? Am I a flying squirrel or a
butterfly?

必須要離開假相，才能知道最初的真相。
也就是，你要先瞭解一切苦、空、無常、無我的道理，
才能夠慢慢離開這些假相，而真相就由此出現。

Only when you stop grabbing hold of illusory phenomena, can you see into the true meaning of the primal truth.
You must first and foremost understand the meaning of suffering, emptiness, impermanence, and selflessness of life in the universe.
Only then can you stay far away from illusory phenomena and get the ultimate truth.

◆二 面對事情的態度
Attitude toward Life

不讓煩惱進來，平常心面對生活、面對工作，
以剔透的心，讓你內心的想法回歸自由，過明覺的生活。

Don't worry, man! Use your 'ordinary mind' to face your life and work.
Also use a clear mind to free your thoughts deep inside and to lead a life
of wisdom.

海水與浪濤 Ocean and Tides

不動如山，煩惱不沾。

Be immovable as a mountain, and vexations will not
fetter you.

生活有時平順，有時波濤洶湧，
就像海水，有時高有時低，
但是無論高或低，
海水依舊是海水。

Life is full of ups and downs.
Just like the rise and fall of the tides.
No matter how the tides change, it's still
the ocean.

海水就像是我們的覺性；
而海浪代表起伏不定的生活。
我們的覺性常被生活？起起伏伏的事情所干擾，
但是不管生活怎麼變動，心依舊是心。
唯有以平常心過生活，煩惱才會少。

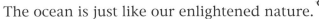

The ocean is just like our enlightened nature.
The rise and fall of the tides is very much like the ups and downs of our life.
Our enlightened nature is always disturbed by these ups and downs in daily life.
No matter how life changes, it's still our original heart.
Just go with our 'ordinary heart', and vexations will dimish.

放它一馬 Let Go

放下執著，同時也放過自己一馬。

Stop clinging and give yourself a break!

佛法跟一般世間的學問不一樣，
它是一切能空的智慧。

Buddha Dharma is different from worldly knowledge.
Buddha Dharma teaches us the wisdom of emptiness.

但是一切皆空並不是什麼都沒有，
而是讓你內心的想法回歸自由，
讓一切的發生怎麼來、怎麼去，
放它一馬，
同時你也放過了你自己。

Emptiness doesn't mean there's nothing at all.
Emptiness brings you back to the original freedom
of your mind and heart.
Things come and go in our life. So, let them come
and go in their own way.
No more clinging, but just let go.
Stop clinging and give yourself a break!

爬高山 Mountain Climbing

「學佛山」爬得愈高，心性愈清明。

Learning Buddha Dharma is like climbing a mountain. The higher you climb, the clearer the air is. The more Buddha Dharm you learn, the clearer your mind will be.

學佛就如同爬高山，
要慢慢地爬，
爬到明心見性的高峰後，再下山。

Learning Buddha Dharma is like climbing a mountain.
Climb slowly until you reach the summit of 'enlightened mind'
and 'original nature'.
It's all downhill after that.

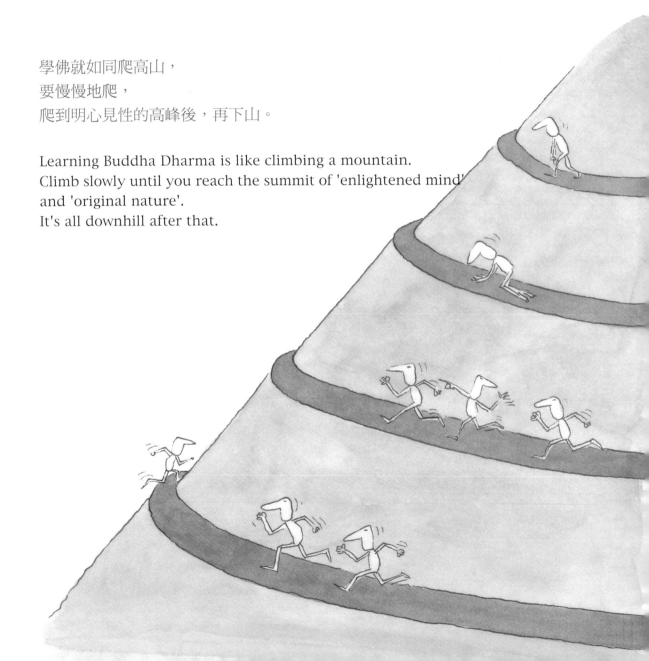

明心見性的人，
就像站在高山上，
看得遠，看得清楚。

The one who realizes the enlightened mind and sees into the
original nature can look far and clear into the distance.

水晶球與鏡子 Crystal Ball and Mirror

有剔透的心，才有無上的智慧。

If you have a crystal clear mind, you can attain the absolute perfect wisdom.

我們這個心，
就像水晶球一樣地，晶瑩剔透，
雖處處應緣而現，
但水晶的本質，依然不變，
這就叫智慧；

Our mind is as clear as a crystal ball that reflects everything it meets.
Still, the crystal ball is a crystal ball.
Nothing changes. That's wisdom.

如果把一面鏡子擺在那邊，
然後照著鏡外的事物一直不動，
這叫做昧，而不是智慧。

Standing a mirror in one place and shining it on objects without
moving is ignorance, not wisdom.

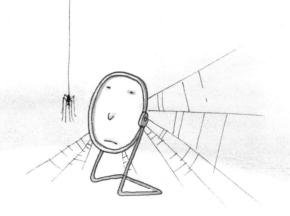

面對挑戰
Facing a Challenge

怎樣才不會產生煩惱？
不要留住煩惱，習慣於釋放煩惱、面對挑戰，
煩惱就不會存在。

How can you be free of vexations?
Don't hide any vexations! You have to let your vexations go, and
face a challenge! Then you'll be free of vexations.

思想排水溝 Drainage of Thought

幫煩惱找一條通道，讓它沒有機會停留。

Find a 'drainage channel' for your vexations and let them all go down the drain.

我們的思緒若是亂糟糟的，就會發生問題；
必須把思緒整理妥當，讓它像排水溝一樣，
有自己的通道，

If your thoughts are confused, your life will
be in a real mess.
You have to collect your thoughts, or build
'drainage systems' as an outlet for vexations.

那麼，當問題來臨時，
就會像雨水流入暢通的排水溝中，
根本不必擔心水會滿溢出來，釀成災害！

When problems arise, it's just like rainwater
flowing unobstructed through the drainage
channels. There's no need to worry about the
water overflowing and causing
a flood or other disasters.

暢通的思緒就如同暢通的排水溝，
沒有垃圾堆積，不會造成阻塞，
也就不會產生煩惱。

A clear mind is just like an unobstructed drainage system, which are in perfect working order.
If there's no garbage piling up, the drainage pipes will be working normally with no clogging.
Then you won't have any vexations.

影子 Shadow

煩惱如同下雨，當雨過天晴，雨復何在？

Vexations are like raining. When the rain stops, the sky clears again, how could there still be rain?

我們的內心，不要去儲藏煩惱的記憶，
要讓煩惱像流水一樣流過去，
隨時使自己變成一個很新鮮的人，
沒有煩惱、沒有陰影。

Don't keep the memories of vexations in your mind.
Let your vexations drain away like flowing water.
Always keep yourself 'refreshed', and there'll be no vexations and
gloom.

固執的人常常煩惱，因為他老停在那裡不動，
其實，煩惱只是一個過路的影子，
你不留住它，它也不可能存在。

A stubborn person often has vexations because he stagnates and refuses to change.
Actually, vexations are just like a passing shadow. They cease to exist if you don't hold on to them.

如少水魚 A fish in Shallow Water

執著身外之物，永不知足；傾聽心內天籟，乃大滿足。

If you cling to external objects, you'll never be satisfied. Listen carefully to the music of nature deep inside your heart and this will be greatly fulfilling.

生活像流水，
忙忙碌碌、急急躁躁，
一天就這樣地過了，
自己到底在做什麼呢？

Life is very much like flowing water.
Hustle and bustle, busily rushing anxiously about.
Just like this, another day goes by.
What on earth am I doing?

我們像魚一樣，
忙碌地在水裡面游來游去，
東啃啃西吃吃，不知不覺生命就完蛋了，
這其中能找到什麼呢？

We're just like fish, busily swimming to-and-fro.
Chomping and eating everywhere without realizing that the end of their lives isn't far. What is to be found in all this?

自己的存在，不在外面，
外面是那麼地患得患失，
因為好也是患得患失，
壞也是苦空無常，
能抓得住什麼呢？
或多或少的錢財和愛欲，
就是這樣來、那樣去，
然而，內在的那份美好，
你曾經嘗試過嗎？

Your true self isn't outside your mind and heart.
The world outside your mind and heart is full of ups and downs.
Maybe you're a born loser. However, you may get something one day.
Or, you get everything you want today. But, you may lose everything you own the next morning.
Still, you can't grab hold of anything in the end!
Possessions come and go, just like money and passion.
Only the peaceful feelings deep inside your mind and heart last forever.
Have you ever tried to touch these feelings?

造反 Revolt

烦惱橫行，造反有理。

Vexations bully us everywhere. Therefore, we have
the right to rebel against them.

我們經常順著煩惱走，
放縱內心生起的貪、瞋、癡，
將我們淹沒，
我們應該要向煩惱造反，
這種造反是有理、是必要的，
因為我們不能被煩惱控制。

We 'go along with' vexations all the time.
Give a loose rein to greed, hatred, and ignorance.
We're dominated by these 'three original vexations'.
We ought to fight back.
Therefore, it's necessary to rebel against them. We also have the right to do that.
We shouldn't be governed by vexations.

四 身體是誰的
Who Really Own This Body?

身體只是房子，「誰」才是它的主人呢？
當一切都無影無蹤，消失不見的時候，
「我」的真相是？
如果我們的心能夠明覺，整個身心就會因此而明亮。

The physical body is only a 'house'. Who's its owner?
All things come and go, vanishing into thin air in the end. Then,
what's the truth of 'I'?
If we enlighten our heart, our body and mind will shine brightly.

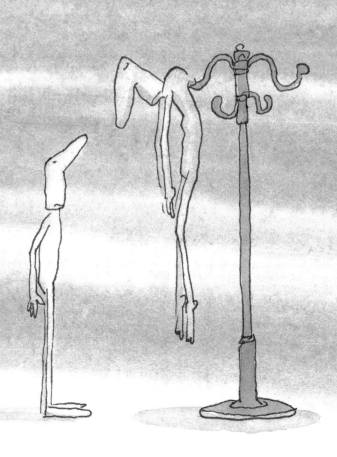

我的真相 The Truth of 'I'

身體只是房子，「我」才是它的主人。

The physical body is only a 'house'. 'I' am its owner.

「我」這個生命，到底是什麼呢？
我們大部分的人，都一直執著這個。
身體就是「我」；如果離開了這個身體，
就不覺得還有什麼東西是「我」。

What's wrong with 'my' life?
Most of us keep on clinging to it.
This body is 'I'.
If you leave your body, you can't feel your own existence.

那究竟父母未生以前，「我」是誰？
死了以後，誰是「我」？
這個身體就像房子一樣，
心臟是辦公室的主機，
五臟六腑是作業單位；
但這房子，誰是主人？
這主人，不是因為擁有這房子，才叫主人，
這主人本來就有的。

Who am 'I' before birth?
Who am 'I' after death?
The body is like an office.
The heart is the director of the office.
Viscera are working units.
However, who is the real owner of the office?
The 'real owner' isn't the one who owns the office.
The 'real owner' himself is his owner.

臭蟲箱 Smelly Bug Box

不見廬山「真面目」。

Can't see what Lushan Mountain really looks like.

什麼是我們的「本來面目」？
其實我們的身體，就是一個臭蟲箱罷了。
身體死了三天就長蟲了，
這不就是臭蟲箱嗎？

What is the 'original face'?
Indeed, the body is just a smelly bug box!
Three days after a person dies the corpse will be full of maggots.
No doubt your body is a smelly bug box!

而我們常常覺得面子很珍貴，臉蛋又那麼重要，
結果被蟲吃了，
只剩下一把骨頭，
面子變成骷顱頭，
再過幾年，火一燒，變成灰，
骨頭粉被風一吹，灑得滿地都是，
一切的尊嚴、高貴、漂亮，全完蛋了！
你看，所執著的一切，
就這麼清潔溜溜了，
所以，為什麼不找真的「本來面目」呢？

You care about your appearance all the time.
When you die, maggots will eat your body leaving only a pile of bones.
Maybe a few years later these bones will be burned to ashes, vanishing into thin air in the end.
All your dignity, nobility, and beauty will completely die out!
All things to which you cling turn to nothingness eventually.
So, why don't you find your true 'original face'?

馬桶 Toilet

覺性永遠不死，只是換一個面貌出現。

'Enlightened nature' never dies. It can take different form every time it appears.

我們的身體，
本來就是地、水、火、風四大物質組合而成，

Originally, our bodies are composed of the four elements:
earth, water, fire, and air.

但四大本無，五蘊皆空，
人死的時候，
這個身體就會像一個臭馬桶被丟掉了，

The Four Elements are originally empty.
The Five Aggregates are all empty.
When a person dies, his or her body will be thrown away like a stinking toilet.

我們的覺性、心識離開身體，
丟下這個身體後，
會再去找一個新的四大鑽進去，
我們的覺性常常就這樣改裝了。

When our enlightened nature and mind-heart consciousness leave our bodies, they go find another 'Five Aggregates' and transmigrate into these new bodies.
The enlightened nature always changes its dress and appearance like so.

五 慾望的慈悲

Longing and Compassion

布施與付出時出時進，流通無礙，沒有分別；
慈悲心也要沒有親疏，沒有負擔！這正是一雨普滋，
千山秀色！

Always make a donation and draw no distinction among all sentient
beings. Have compassion for all living beings. That's exactly like the
timely rain falling on the dried earth, irrigating all vegetation equally.
All plants and trees grow vigorously and beautifully in the mountains
then!

水庫 Reservoir

愛心流出去，快樂流進來。

Love flows through me to all sentient beings, and happiness will come into my life.

布施和付出，
就像水庫中的水，
有進才有出，有出才有進。

Donating and giving are like the waters of a reservoir, flowing in and out intermittently.

如果你一直留著它，
它就流不出去，
既然舊的流不出去，
也就裝不下新的。

If you keep the water and don't let it flow
out, the 'old water' can't drain away and
the 'new water' will never fill the reservoir.

所以，要時出時進，流通無礙，
才能保鮮，
也才不會成為一池臭水。

So, always let the water in the reservoir flow unimpeded.
Keep the water clean and flowing, and there will be no stinking water.

回收 Cause and Effect

學佛學一個道理：心種其因，身受其果。

Learning Buddha Dharma is to understand the principle of cause and effect.

學佛後就要懂得因果的道理，
而因果，就是相信無論自己做什麼事，
最後終會有一個回收。

Learning Buddha Dharma is to understand the principle of cause and effect.
Whatever you do, you will receive the appropriate results of your own doing.

如果，你常常觀察這種回收的道理，
那就會明白：
自己想要回收什麼，
自己應該要做什麼！

If you take stock of this principle of cause and effect all the time, you will understand what you want to do next!

賺錢與用錢 Making, Saving, and Spending Money

任何人都有慾望，我們的慾望如果是成佛，
天下就太平了。

Everybody has desires. If we have an overwhelming desire
to become a Buddha, we'll have a real peaceful world.

慾望是一切的開始，
有負擔的慾望就會累，
沒有負擔的慾望就很好，
所以，慾望並不可怕，
重要的是，要知道如何運用、分配，

Desire is the origin of all good and evil matter.
Desire with a tremendous burden will wear you out.
However, desire with no burden is not bad for you.
So, desires aren't all terrible!
Doing everything in moderation is the most important thing.

就像有錢並不是罪惡，
學會支配金錢的技巧，把它用在善行義舉上，
才是發揮了金錢的最大價值。

It's not a sin to be rich.
Learn to manage money skillfully and make charitable donations.
That's the way to get the most value out of your money.

照顧身體 Take Care of Your Body

慈悲心沒有親疏、不分你我，與眾生同呼吸。

A 'Compassionate Heart' makes no distinction between relatives and strangers, or between you and me.
We show a Great Compassionate Heart towards all sentient beings.

一般人的慈悲，
只是應付式的、生滅性的。

Most people show compassion for others superficially.

真正慈悲的人，
對待眾生就像自己和身體的關係，
不論身體冷了、痛了，
只要一點點傷害，都會盡力去保護它。
明心見性的人，
乃是徹底地知道眾生的痛癢。
因為整個宇宙都跟他有關係，
所以說：「同體大悲」。

A real compassionate person treats all living beings as his or her own body.

If his or her body is in pain and feels cold, or hurts a bit, he or she will care for this body wholeheartedly.

The one who realizes the enlightened mind and sees into the original nature can thoroughly understand the suffering of all sentient beings.

It's because the enlightened one is closely connected with the whole universe.

That's to say: "great compassion embraces all beings".

起心動念
Thoughts Arising

生活中佛法無處不在，觀察念頭何時起何時滅，
明白有與空以後，你會充滿喜樂，讓生命更充實！
漸漸地，你就能感受快樂，明白本來面目！

Buddha Dharma is everywhere in everyday life.
Observe when thoughts are arising and fading away.
When you grasp the meaning of existence and emptiness, you'll lead
a full and happy life!
You'll gradually appreciate happiness in life, and comprehend the
'original face'!

擁有 Possessions

「有」讓我們牽掛，「空」才能清淨無憂。

We always feel uneasy about our 'possessions'.
Only 'emptiness' can bring us the serene tranquility and peacefulness.

擁有，能讓你感到滿足嗎？能讓你的生命更充實嗎？

不見得如此吧！

如果你想擁有某個東西，

念頭一動，煩惱就隨之而來，

因為，一旦我們擁有某樣東西，心中就有了牽掛，

怕它有什麼閃失，因此就必須花費精神照顧它，

這就成了你的負擔。

Can 'possessions' satisfy your desires and answer your needs in life?

I doubt it!

Things you want spring to mind. Vexations will then be right around the corner.

Once you have those things, you'll be anxious about losing them.

You have to watch it carefully, so as not to suffer loss of it. It'll take lots of time and energy.

That's your heavy burden.

不論是事業、家庭、親人，都是如此。
因此，唯有擁有一顆明白的心，才是最快樂的。
在世間所擁有的一切，就像手中捧滿的水，
終究會流失、漏乾。
即使得到了也會失去，這就是空。

It won't matter if you have a career and family. All of these are your terrible burdens.
So, the most joyful thing in the world is to have a 'clear mind'.
All things you possess in the mundane world are just like the water you're holding in the palms of your hands.
The water will be dripping away.
Whatever you get, you'll lose.
That's the truth of emptiness.

迴照本來 Reflect on the Original Source

無我，真我原本一物。

Selflessness and true self are the same thing originally.

有一個東西，在控制我們的身體，
就像機器要開啟電源才會動；
那個無形的東西，控制著身體的一切，
現在、過去、未來，都是同一個東西。

Something controls the body.
It's just like the main power of a machine.
This unseen thing controls the whole body.
Whenever past, present, and future, it's the same thing.

打坐，可以靜靜地察覺，
那個東西的面貌，
漸漸地，你明瞭了自己，
可能叫做無我、真我、本來面目，
或是叫做佛、上帝，
也可能是阿拉。

Sitting in meditation lets you see into the appearance of this un-
seen thing.
Gradually, you penetrate the ultimate truth of yourself.
You can call it selflessness, true self, or original face.
Moreover, you can also call it Buddha, God, or Allah!

身體大宮殿 Splendid Palace of the Body

無欲則安，無求乃樂。

Moderate your desire and you will lead a peaceful life.
Whatever you do, relax and ease your mind and your body will lead
a joyful life.

身體就像是一座宮殿，
心就住在這裡面，它是佛，也是魔。
怎麼說呢？
正知正見叫做「佛」，邪知邪見叫做「魔」，

Your body is like a palace, and your mind dwells therein.
The mind is a Buddha, and also a demon.
Why?
If you grasp right understanding, you're a Buddha.
If you have the wrong and foul understanding, you're a demon.

佛與魔都是心的作用，
所以，如果心能夠明覺，整個宮殿就會因此而明亮；
如果心不能明覺，這座身體大宮殿就會變得黯淡無光。

The mind has the potential to become a Buddha or a demon.
If the mind is awakened, the whole palace will be shining and
blazing brightly.
If the mind isn't awakened, the splendid palace of the body will
be dim and gloomy.

魚游 Fish in the Water

魚不知水，魚才自在；放下執著，何其自在。

Fish pay no attention to the water, and can lead a relaxed and a peaceful life.
Let go of your attachment and you can have a serene life!

懂得佛法的人，
要在起心動念處觀空，
觀空不是什麼都沒有，
而是使自己生活得更逍遙自在，

The one who knows Buddha Dharma will meditate on empti-
ness when thoughts are arising and fading away.
Emptiness doesn't mean nothingness.
Meditating on emptiness can help you to lead a serene life.

就像魚在大海中，自由自在地游來游去，
卻不分別那是大海。

It's just like fish in the ocean, swimming about freely and tranquilly.
Those fish won't keep grabbing hold of the idea of the ocean.

七 心靈爆米花

Popcorn Popping of Our Heart

修行就像工作一樣，別忘了你是誰？
別忘了你在幹什麼？
實事求是，腳踏實地循階而上，
才能體會生活即菩提！

Spiritual practice is like doing a job. Don't forget who you are! Don't forget what you're doing! Learn how to stand on your own two feet. Search out the truth step by step, and you will realize daily life is enlightened life.

爆米花 Popcorn Popping

混亂的心像在爆米花，禪修可以讓它平靜、有味。

Confused mind is like popping popcorn.
Practicing Zen can ease the confused mind.

心的念頭就像爆玉米花，
霹靂啪啦，想東想西，
沒有辦法靜下來，
如此一來，
對很多事情也就無法細細體會。

Twisted thoughts from your mind are just like popping popcorn.
You're annoyed about the crackling of popcorn popping.
You're unable to calm down and think clearly.
Then your mind isn't clear enough to see into the things.

因為，粗糙的心，

無法想得很細膩，

唯有透過禪修，亂七八糟的心才會靜下來，

就像玉米花爆完後，

就不會再吵了。

It's because a 'coarse mind' can't think clearly and distinctly.
Only practicing Zen can clear up your muddy thinking and
calm yourself.
When popcorn popping is over, it'll be quiet again.

淌混水 Turbid Water

禪修是心靈的淨水器。

Practicing Zen is just like the water purifier of mind and heart.

我們在忙碌而疲累時，
心就像淌了一趟混水而變混濁了。
但透過禪修以後，
本來很混濁的水，
就會變得非常清澈、平靜、祥和。

When we're toiling away all day and feel tired out; it's like turbid water soaking through our mind and heart. The turbid water will 'pollute' our mind and heart. Practicing Zen can purify the polluted water. After this purification the water will be clear, limpid, and tranquil.

這時，
再多的煩惱、不協調，
來到這個平靜之湖，
都會變得非常平靜。

Then,
this tranquil lake can still all vexations and
incongruity.

打子彈 Shooting

修行是修心，心在哪裡？靶在哪裡？

Spiritual practice is to cultivate the heart.
Where is the heart? Where is the target?

修行如果不瞄準靶心，
永遠就像瞎子打子彈一樣，
哪裡會中呢？

If spiritual practice doesn't take aim at the bull's-eye, you'll shoot bullets
like the blind.
You'll never hit the target!

即使修一百個法、一萬個法，
會不會打中，還是問題呢！
千萬不要亂打一氣，
要打中靶心，抓住修行的核心。

Perhaps you have a hundred, or even ten thousand methods of
spiritual practice.
However, the problem is whether or not you can hit the target!
Don't shoot at the wrong target!
You should hit the bull's-eye.
You have to grasp the core meaning of spiritual practice.

小人物狂想曲 A Cipher's Rhapsody

修行就是上樓梯，不要妄想一步登天，
要腳踏實地，一步一腳印。

Spiritual cultivation is just like walking up the stairs. You have to stand on
your own two feet. Do things step by step, and you will grasp the meaning
of life one day.

修行就是在工作裡、生活裡，
隨時隨地能夠省察自己、反省自己，
工作的時候，別忘了你是誰？
生活的時候，別忘了你在幹什麼？

Practice spiritual Cultivation in your daily job and everyday
life.
Be introspective all the time.
Never forget who are you when you work!
Never forget what are you doing when you live your life!

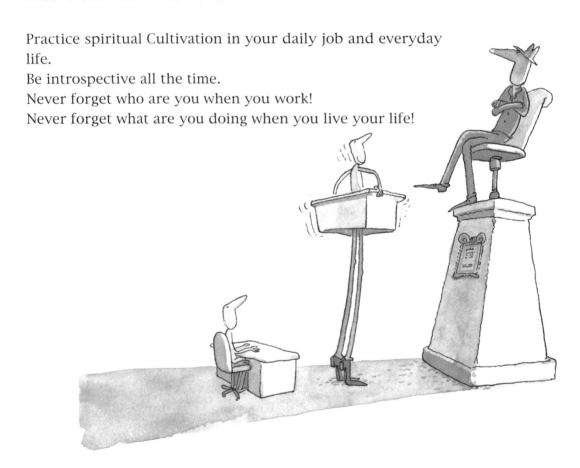

小人物常常作狂想曲，
整天喜歡大成就，
看不到自己的樓梯在哪裡？
忘了生活中，要實事求是，
生活即菩提。

Ciphers always like to compose rhapsodies.
They want a great achievement overnight.
They don't understand how to stand on their own two feet.
Search for the truth step by step in daily life.
Everyday life is enlightened life.

八 管控自己的心念

Managing Your Own Mind

一念清淨即清淨，一念無明即無明。
懂得消化煩惱，便能讓生活自在逍遙，讓生命更寬廣。

When a good thought arises, all thoughts are good.
When a bad thought arises, all thoughts are bad.
If you let go of vexations, you'll lead a free and easy life.

扇子 Fan

懂得調心，就像擁有一把搧盡煩憂的大扇子。

For one who knows how to manage the mind, it's just like he or she possesses a huge fan that can blow out the fire of vexations.

無明生起時，用扇子把它搧開，
像是熱了就開電扇，把熱氣吹散，

When ignorance arises, blow it away.
It's just like when you feel hot, you turn on the fan.

人間不是天堂，也不是地獄，
常常會有快樂，也會有痛苦！

Our mundane world is neither heaven nor hell.
There's often both happiness and suffering in the worldly world.

所以，我們要學習怎麼調心，
把心調到安定、無煩惱。

We need to learn how to manage our mind.
If we manage our mind successfully, we'll be serene and free
from vexations.

放牛吃草 Release a Cow and Let It Graze

一念之間，成佛成魔；一念之間，為善為惡。

You have to make your own decision. You can be a Buddha or you can be a demon. You can also decide to be good or to be evil. You have to decide for yourself. The future is in your own hands.

把自己的心管好，
不要污染、不要害人……，
更不要生出很多亂七八糟的想法。

Gain good control over the mind.
Don't pollute your mind. Don't do harm to others...
Besides, don't let evil thoughts arise.

一念清淨即清淨，
一念無明即無明，
念念都可以讓人墮落，
也可以讓人超生，提升

One clean and pure thought having arisen will purify all thoughts.
One muddy and polluted thought having arisen will pollute all thoughts.
One single evil thought can corrupt your life.
One single good thought can uplift your life.

所以，要隨時管控自己的心念，
心念管不好，
就像放牛吃草，
任牠亂吃一通，製造問題。

So, do gain good control over the mind all the time.
If you don't manage this well, it'll be like releasing a
cow and letting it graze without limit.
It will harm the cow, and create more problems.

小孩的玩頭 Kids Play

專心吃飯專心玩；專心禪修專心定！

Concentrate on eating and playing.
Concentrate on Zen meditating, and concentrate the mind!

我們的心，飄忽不定，
如何讓這個飄忽的心，能夠停下來呢？
就是要訓練心的專一。
念咒專心念咒、禪修專心禪修、看經專心看經，
這都是做一種專一的工作。

The mind is always wondering and horsing around.
What can we do to concentrate the mind?
Let's concentrate our mind!
Concentrate on reciting mantra, Zen meditating, and reading Sutras.
All these are concentration practicing.

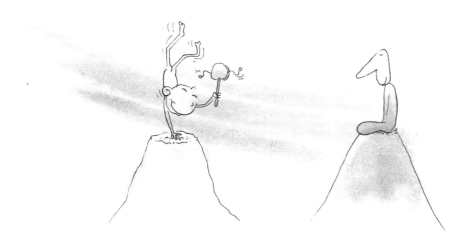

心就像小孩一樣，很難管，
但，小孩子有了玩頭以後，就不會調皮了，
所以，心要讓它有玩頭。

The mind, just like a frolicsome child, is not easy to take in hand.
When the child is absorbed in playing a particular thing, he'll no
longer be horsing around.
So, let our mind be absorbed in some things too.

要玩什麼呢？
就是玩怎麼樣讓自己的心喜歡「定」，
要讓它定在心性上、佛性上，
也就是定在真理上。

What things should we play?
Let's play concentrating.
Concentrate on the mind and the Buddha nature.
That means concentrate on the ultimate truth.

導火線 Fuse

找到心的所在，就能悟出世間的真理。

Digging up where the 'heart' is and you can comprehend the truth of 'supramundanity'.

心是一切能源的所在，
一切的問題，導火線就是心，
它能感受痛苦，也能感受快樂，
它會製造煩惱，也能明白世間的無常與矛盾，
所以，我們必須找到心的所在，
才能悟到永恆不變的真理。

Our heart is the source of all energy.
It's also the 'explosive fuse' of all problems.
It feels pain and also gets pleasure.
It creates vexations. However, it can realize the unsureness and contradictions
of the worldly world.
So, we have to uncover the heart and grasp the meaning of the ultimate truth.

心靈舞蹈 Heart Dancing

行也禪，坐也禪，語默動靜體安然。

When we walk, we practice Zen. When we sit, we practice Zen.
When we speak or listen, run fast or sit still, we also practice Zen
tranquilly and peacefully.

禪就像舞蹈一樣，
你可以把心靈的想法跳出來，
也可以將內心的感受表現出來，與大家分享，
讓別人感受到你那份內在。
禪就是生活、就是心，
我們的日常生活，
就像跳一場心靈的舞蹈。

Zen is very much like dancing.
When you dance, you can express yourself.
Expressing what you really think deep in your heart.
Let somebody know what you really feel.
Zen is our everyday life. Zen is our heart.
Our daily life is just like a show of heart dancing.

心的方向盤

'Steering Wheel' of the Heart

遇到困境時，握緊心的方向盤，用智慧來轉化；
把阻礙化為力量，轉個念頭，心境才會敞開！

When you run into difficulty, just grab the 'steering wheel' of your heart.

Turn this difficulty into power with wisdom.

If you change your mind about the difficulty, you'll feel much better!

亂流 Turbulence

亂流來時，要握緊心的方向盤。

When 'turbulence' comes, just grab the 'steering wheel' of the heart.

飛機在天上飛的時候，
亂流一來，飛機也許會出事，這是很危險的。

When airplanes fly into turbulence, it's very dangerous.

當我們的心混亂的時候，
就像亂流通過！
心會開始失調，
甚至離開安全航道而墜落。
所以，要小心這股亂流呀！

When our heart is in chaos, it's just like it hits
turbulence, everything is out of control; our heart
may 'fly off' the 'flight path' and 'crash' then!

轉一轉 One More Changing

念頭在心頭，不舒服；轉個念頭，心頭就開。

When something in your mind makes you feel uncomfortable, just change your mind about the matter and you'll feel comfortable.

遇到困境時，我們要試著把意識轉開，
彷彿，我們已經不在境相中，
如此，心境就會好轉。

When we run into trouble, just try to put it out of our consciousness,
let's make believe the trouble bugs out.
We'll feel much better then!

譬如說，吃不到蛋糕時，
就不要一直想著吃蛋糕！
改吃別的吧！花生也好、水果也好，
只要學會把念頭轉一轉，
事情就會跟著好轉了。

For example, when you can't have the cake you want,
just don't think about it.
Eat something different. Salted peanuts are okay, some
fruit is also all right!
Just learn to have an agile mind and change your thinking whenever the need arises.
Things will go all right then!

紅塵大海 Ocean of the Mundane World

不怕驚濤駭浪，只怕道心不堅。

Although the perils of life are like the perils of the ocean, it's not terrible. We're not chickenhearted. However, I'm afraid of the vanishing of the enlightened heart.

我們能超越物質，乃因明覺的關係，
所以，要能夠隨時隨地醒悟、省察執著和妄想。
如果連這種基本的訓練都沒有，
就容易迷失在紛擾的紅塵中，

We can transcend the material world because of the enlightened mind.
Therefore, be awakened and examine your thoughts all the time.
If you don't have such basic training, you'll easily get lost in this turbulent mundane world.

就像大海什麼時候要吞滅我們，不知道！
這紅塵大海吞滅我們，是連渣都不剩的，
所以要常高掛警覺的心、審思的心，
讓自己擁有堅固的道心，來實踐佛法。

It's just like the ocean which may 'devour' us anytime
without leaving a trace.
Maybe we'll be completely submerged by this 'worldly
ocean' some day.
So, we have to remain vigilant all the time.
Let's have a strong 'enlightened heart', and practice
Buddha's teachings faithfully.

糖入水 Sugar in the Water

心常融於虛空，阻礙消失無蹤。

Once the heart 'merge into' emptiness, all hurdles will be cleared.

在生活中，
如果要把阻礙化為一股力量，就要學習包容，

In everyday life,
if you want to convert obstacles into a torrent of power, you need to learn
how to be tolerant.

用空性的智慧來轉化，讓心常保持在虛空的狀態，
即任何東西加入虛空中，對於虛空都沒有影響。
那麼，任何事事物物來到我們的身邊時，
就像是糖掉入水裡，
一會兒就溶化，消失於無形了。

Use the wisdom of emptiness to transform difficulties in life.
Let the mind be always in the state of emptiness.
No matter what problems 'emptiness' may encounter, still, 'emptiness' is emptiness; nothing can affect it.
Then, anything that comes our way, just like sugar melting into the water, will vanish into thin air.

閃閃發光的心

The Glittering Heart

一個具足真理的人，就像天上的星星，
那麼地閃亮，一直放射能量；
學佛使每一個人，
都能找回自己那顆閃閃發光的心。

Originally, everyone knows the ultimate truth. It's just like the glittering stars in the sky, radiating energy endlessly.
Learning Buddha's teachings can help us to regain our 'glittering heart'.

星星 Stars

「心」際導航，探索生命的奧秘！

The 'Heart Flight' is navigating the secret of life!

每個人的心，
都像天上的星星一樣，
是那麼地閃亮；
如果我們的心被蒙蔽了，
就感覺到煩惱與無明的黑暗，
學佛就是找回自己這一顆心！
使每一個人，都有一顆閃閃發光的心，
學佛，就是學著拭去塵埃。

Our heart is originally very much like the glittering stars in the sky.
If our heart is bamboozled or 'covered up', we'll experience the darkness of vexations and ignorance.
Learning Buddha's teachings can help us to find this lost 'true heart'!
Everybody, then, can regain the 'glittering heart'.
Learning Buddha's teachings is learning to dust the dust off the 'true heart'.

拜師學藝 Learn from Your Master

以佛為師，才知道法無疆界。

Learning from Buddha and you'll realize the boundlessnesss of the Dharma World.

知道宇宙生命的真理，
我們才會知道生命之旅。
怎麼走、怎麼開，路線在哪裡，
慢慢地除了開車外，
飛機也會開，太空船也會開，
所有交通工具都會開了，
此時，便能了知生命路線的方向，
以及宇宙有什麼好玩。

Once you see into the truth of the 'universal life', you know the meaning of the journey through life.
How to go? How to drive? Where's the route of your life?
Gradually, you learn how to drive a car, airplane, spacecraft etc.
Then, you manage to drive all kinds of 'vehicles of life', and understand the direction and route of your life.
Also, you'll get to know the interesting things in the universe.

如果你還不知道，
就要拜佛為師，
向佛學習正確的方法，
才知道怎麼走、怎麼玩；
不學佛法，
怎麼走也只是走在輪迴這條路上，
走不出地球以外的地方了。

If you don't know yet, just follow the Buddha's teachings.
Learn from Buddha and you'll know the direction you go and the
way you play.
If you don't learn Buddha Dharma, no matter how you go and
what you do, you're still on the road to reincarnation.
And you'll never leave this mundane world!

想要走出地球以外的世界，
就要學佛、皈依三寶，
到時候，自然知道法界無疆界。

If you want to go away from the mundane world, you
have to learn the Buddha's teachings, and take refuge
in the Three Jewels.
Naturally, you'll comprehend the boundlessness of the
Dharma World at that time.

敞開空門 Open the Door of Emptiness

打開空門，讓生命延伸出去。

Open the door of emptiness and broaden your horizons.

原本我們的心就不停地製造空間，以便有活動的場所，

但是，心若不能覺悟，就無法製造空間讓我們活動。

也就是說，心愈狹隘，活動的空間就愈窄，

如同有些人很有錢，心卻很閉塞，

因為他已被錢的表相，堵得走投無路了。

Originally, the heart makes space for our activities.

If the heart is covered up or unenlightened, there'll be no space for activity.

That's to say a narrow mind gives you a narrow space.

Some rich people, for example, have the narrowest mind.

It's because money has blocked their road to enlightenment.

They've no way to go!

所以，佛打開空門給我們走，就是要讓我們的生命更寬廣。
只要不執著於幻相，
便能打開空門，自在逍遙的生活。

Therefore, Buddha opens the door of emptiness for us, and broadens our life.
Don't grab hold of illusory phenomena, and we can open the door of emptiness and lead an easy tranquil life.

太陽能 Solar Energy

學佛幫我們找回生命本來具足的能量。

Learning Buddha's teachings can help us to find out the original energy of life.

太陽是一顆不斷放射光芒的星球，
雖然它不曉得自己做了什麼，
但是，很多生物都因為它的光，而產生活力；

The sun radiates heat and light endlessly.
Although the sun emits heat and light completely
unawares, lots of living beings benefit from it, and
have energy because of it.

一個具足真理的人就像太陽，

一直放射能量，

雖然你未曾察覺，

但是，許多人卻因為你的存在，而得到滋潤。

學佛可以幫助我們找回真理，

找回本來具足的能量。

A man who grasps the meaning of ultimate truth is very much like the sun, radiating 'energy' unawares.

Lots of people benefit from him.

Learning Buddha's teachings can help us to find out the ultimate truth, and regain our 'original abundant energy'.

國家圖書館出版品預行編目資料

心靈舞蹈／心道法師作；尤傳賢繪圖；
　　許國華英譯.-- 初版.-- 臺北市：靈鷲山出版，
　　2001〔民90〕
　　　面；　　公分.--（心道法師系列；4）

　　　ISBN 957-99025-4-2（平裝）

　1. 勵志　2.心理　3.佛教

　225.79　　　　　　　　　90017785

Mind Ballet